NEW ENGLAND LANDMARKS

THE PORT OF
GLOUCESTER

Christmas 03

All the Best —
Come Visit in '04

Dan

Photographs by Josh Reynolds

Commonwealth Editions
Beverly, Massachusetts

The author gratefully acknowledges the *Gloucester Daily Times* for its kind permission to use photographs originally published in that newspaper.

International Standard Book Number: 1-889833-17-7

Designed by Bonnie McGrath.
Printed in South Korea.

Commonwealth Editions is an imprint of
Memoirs Unlimited, Inc., 21 Lothrop Street,
Beverly, Massachusetts 01915

Visit our web site: www.commonwealtheditions.com.

To order prints of individual photos visit:
www.joshreynoldsphoto.com.

Foreword

When I first heard the name Howard Blackburn, I asked what his contribution to Gloucester had been. I was told, "His hands." Blackburn lost his frostbitten fingers rowing himself and a dead dorymate to Newfoundland from Burgeo Bank. He is a fitting hero for a city whose fame and fortune have come at the cost of those who went to sea but did not come back.

Gloucester claims to be not only America's oldest fishing port but also home of the nation's oldest artists' colony. Generations have been lured to its shores, navigating by Cape Ann's lighthouses and also painting them. Writing of them, too. From Rudyard Kipling to Sebastian Junger, Fitz Hugh Lane to Howard Kline, Charles Olsen to Peter Prybot, Henry Ferrini to Joe Garland, Milton Avery to Nubar Alexanian, Daisy Nell to Nell Blain—the work of authors and artists has made Gloucester famous far beyond its size. Whether interested in sailors or sunbathers, each has responded to things seen and stories told. In this respect, they are all journalists.

The pictures in this book fit a stricter definition of journalism. They are an attempt to show what life was like in the port of Gloucester in the closing years of the twentieth century. Today tensions run high as Gloucester's scenic shores attract developers, prompting fishermen and activists to take up arms in defense of the working waterfront, even as some of the choicest locations sit crumbling or vacant. To the consternation of many, as fish stocks dwindle and government regulations tighten, casino boats cruise into town and make their haul twice daily by allowing passengers to fish in their own pockets.

Still, almost four centuries since the city's founding in 1623 and nearly a century past the great age of the fishing schooners, Gloucester retains its noble heritage as a haven for fishermen and artists alike.

—Josh Reynolds, April 2000

This book is dedicated to the memory of former *Gloucester Daily Times* photographer Charles Lowe. Though he preceded me by two decades, it was rare for me to receive a compliment that was not also an unfavorable comparison to him. His work has been both a challenge and an inspiration.

A dory rower glides across the inner harbor past a backdrop of City Hall and St. Ann's Church.

Escorted by a squadron of hungry gulls, the dragger St. Mary steams past Eastern Point Light with a haul of fish. White-tipped orange masts, probably a combination of Portuguese tradition and Coast Guard requests for higher visibility, once characterized the Gloucester fishing fleet.

Cod landings, once a staple of the coastal economy, dropped precipitously in the 1990s. In 1990 local boats netted 22 million pounds. By 1995 that number had fallen to 5.4 million. In early 1999 the government closed fishing grounds and imposed severe catch limits. Regulators called the effort a success, but fishermen were dismayed that the limits forced them to discard thousands of pounds of fish caught in open grounds. Most of the fish died in the nets and were tossed overboard.

Above: *The Coast Guard ferries food out to the looming Russian freezer ship* Babrungas. *The crew refused to work until their captain secured food other than the herring that the ship had purchased from Gloucester vessels for transport to Russia.*

Right: *A small-boat fisherman loads buckets to be hauled out of the hold at trip's end.*

Far left: *A fish buyer samples a recently landed tuna. Buyers taste a strip cut from the tail and inspect the fat and oil content of the fish before offering a price.*

Left: *A cutter dresses a 388-pound bluefin at Cape Ann Tuna. Tuna bring high prices, and the choicest are packed on ice and air-freighted to Japan to be served fresh as sushi.*

A pair of patrons embrace at the Crow's Nest, the fishermen's watering hole made famous by Sebastian Junger's book The Perfect Storm. The bar now attracts tour groups and sight-seers.

Since its installation in 1925, Leonard Craske's Man at the Wheel has stood as a monument to those who went to sea and did not return.

KEEP OFF
MONUMENT

Above: *A shipwright works on the exposed ribs of the schooner* Adventure *during restoration in 1998. Built in 1926, the 121-foot dory trawler was the last of her kind to fish the Atlantic.*

Right: *The Essex-built schooner* Roseway, *here seen under repair at Gloucester Marine Railways, once guided ships through Boston Harbor. She now carries passengers out of Camden, Maine.*

Left: *The Mayflower II was hauled out for maintenance at Gloucester Marine Railways in 1999. As fishing business has trickled away, this repair yard has struggled to stay afloat financially. The business has sold one of its sites for conversion to a maritime heritage park.*

Above: *Working to preserve a more recent piece of history, an enthusiast restores his 1920s-vintage Lawley motor launch, built as a commuter shuttle.*

Lane Briggs, organizer of the Chesapeake Bay Schooner Race, pitches in to raise the mainsail on the schooner Harvey Gamage *during Gloucester's annual Mayor's Cup schooner race.*

A crew member stands on the crosstrees of the schooner Lettie G. Howard *during a Mayor's Cup schooner race. The* Howard, the Adventure, *and the* Roseway *are three of only five remaining Essex schooners.*

A summer electrical storm lights up the Cut Bridge on Stacy Boulevard, said to be the busiest drawbridge on the East Coast.

Above: *The aftermath of a summer storm on Pavilion Beach.*

Right: *Sculptor Al Duca's statue of famed seascape painter Fitz Hugh Lane gives a lesson to Gloucester middle school students. The statue was Duca's final work, and he died before the unveiling.*

Left: *This sun worshipper on Wingaersheek Beach was unaware of the persona she assumed while in search of her own movie-star tan.*

Above: *A walking skiff.*

Passengers crowd the pulpit of the Yankee Spirit, one of many charter boats that carry sightseers in search of whales during the summer months. Humpback whales (right) are a common sight on Stellwagen Bank, but the Northern right whale is so close to extinction that attempts have been made to curtail fishing and lobstering off New England during the whale's migratory season.

Above: *Celebrants light candles for the Friday evening procession of St. Peter's Fiesta. The festival honoring the patron saint of fishermen began as a storefront display in the 1920s and now engages the entire city.*

Right: *At the end of Sunday morning's procession, confetti is tossed from the roof of St. Peter's Club.*

Bearers carry the statue of St. Peter to a shrine and two churches as they wend their way along the Sunday parade route.

St. Peter's Fiesta is the official start of summer in Gloucester. The weeklong festival founded by Sicilian immigrants is an unusual mix of carnival and Catholicism that also reflects the town's dangerous livelihood as a seaport. Some celebrate with rosary beads in nightly services; others party in downtown bars, which enjoy their busiest weekend of the year. An annual visit from the cardinal and a blessing of the fleet combine with high spirits and fishing-derived sporting events.

Seine boat crews once race to haul nets around schools of fish. They now race each other in the final sporting event of the fiesta.

A slip from the Greasy Pole can be painful, but walking it on fiesta weekend is an honor that fishermen (and, more recently, their hand-picked substitutes) are eager to accept.

Left: *Nino Sanfilippo tears the flag from the end of the Greasy Pole, claiming the title as 1998 Sunday champion. The Greasy Pole winner swims to shore, but his feet never touch the beach, as fellow competitors hoist him on their shoulders and carry him off to the teeming bars downtown.*

Above: *Our Lady of Fatima.*

Sightseers on an amphibious "duck tour" startle a sunbather on Pavilion Beach, perhaps recalling the documented appearance of a sea serpent off Gloucester in the 1840s.

Clammer David Sargent walks the sand flats on the Essex River in Gloucester. "I'm a hunter-gatherer in an information age," says Sargent, who checks Doppler weather radar via the Internet to anticipate rain closures on the flats.

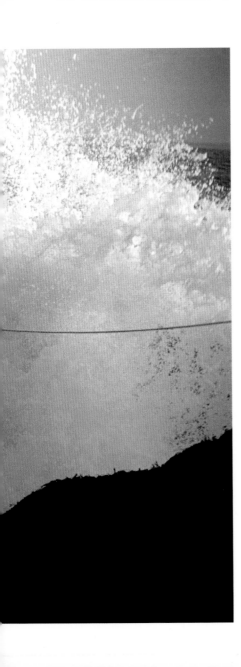

A rescuer comes to the aid of a young surfer stranded by waves crashing on Bass Rocks.

Above: *Fishermen hurry to save their boats from a fire that leveled Fisherman's Wharf in September 1998.*

Left: *An often-painted wood-frame warehouse destroyed by the conflagration was the last of its kind on the waterfront. The owners, a fishing cooperative, began rebuilding the following year.*

Left: *A derelict fishing boat sits at the Frontiero Brothers' wharf in the inner harbor. Maritime law requires the owner to pay for removal. Because of the prohibitive cost, wrecks often tie up useful space for years.*

Above: *Discouraged fishermen play cards at St. Peter's Club. Many were idled by the government's closure of inshore fishing grounds in early 1999.*

Many of the inshore fleet stayed tied to their docks during what would have been prime cod season during the early months of 1999.

Above: *When the* Southern Belle *steamed into town looking for shelter from a passing storm, she raised Gloucester's gambling fleet to four boats. Gambling cruises draw both passengers and criticism. Local law-makers look in vain for a legal way to ban them. Though most passengers are out-of-towners, Gloucester is a gambling town. Per capita lottery sales are the second highest in the state.*

Next page: *Animosity between regulators and fishermen has been building since the 1970s when the first signs of over-fishing resulted in government restrictions. Fishermen accuse regulators of sloppy science and political favoritism, while regulators claim they are simply protecting the future of the fisheries.*

MANDATORY TAGGING OF ALL US CAUGHT BLUEFIN TUNA
MORE
DON'T LET

Right: *A camera operator prepares to shoot a scene for the film version of* The Perfect Storm *in front of Our Lady of Good Voyage Church. The film is the most recent of several memorializing Gloucester fishermen, stretching back to 1937's classic* Captains Courageous.

Next page: *The names of Gloucester fishermen lost at sea grace a stairwell at City Hall.*

1915

CHARLES ANTOIL
JOSEPH BEATON
OLIVER BULLOCK
ROBERT CAVANAUGH
RICHARD COMERFORD
BERNARD CURTIS
JERRY DANIELS
CAPT. ROBERT DIGGINS
LEWIS DIX
HOWARD FEBNER
JOHN GOODWIN
DENNIS HUBBARD
NELS JOHNSON
WILLIAM KALEMAR
PIUS LANDRY
WILLIAM MC CARTHY
ARCHIE MC LEAN
WILLIAM MC NAIR
ARTHUR MC NEIL
PIUS MC PHEE
ALBERT MURPHY
CAPT. ADELBERT NICKERSON
ADELBERT J. NICKERSON
CHARLES R. NICKERSON
OLIVEIRA PERNANDEZ
JOHN PERRY
MANUEL SILVA
JOHN BELL STILLETTO
JOSEPH TEBEDO
WILLIAM WATER
JOHN WORTHING